CONQUEROR'S CACHE®
BOOK THREE:

FAITH
TO
FORGIVE

Christina M. Johnson

TESTIMONY PUBLISHERS, LLC.

Jackson, Wyoming

CONQUEROR'S CACHE® BOOK THREE: FAITH TO FORGIVE

Published by Testimony Publishers, LLC.

DISCLAIMER

This book is intended for informational and inspirational purposes only. Neither the publisher, editor, nor author is engaged in rendering professional advice or services to the individual reader. The ideas, information, exercises, methods, procedures, products, and suggestions contained in this book are not intended as a substitute for consulting with a board-certified physician. All matters regarding the individual reader's health require expert medical advice and supervision. Neither the publisher, editor, nor author shall be liable or responsible for any loss or damage allegedly arising from any idea, information, procedures, and suggestions in this book. Readers are advised to do their own due diligence when it comes to making business decisions and all ideas, information, exercises, methods, procedures, products, and suggestions that have been provided should be independently verified by your own qualified professional. The publisher has used its best endeavors to ensure that the URLs for external websites referred to in this book are correct and active at the time of going to press. However, the publisher and the author have no responsibility for the websites and can make no guarantee that a site will remain live or that the content will remain relevant, decent, or appropriate.

Printed in the United States of America

ISBN: 978-1-7322956-2-9

In addition to book signings, Christina M. Johnson is available for your corporate, conference, church, government agency, non-profit, professional association, and business networking event as a speaker, trainer, or facilitator. Send your requests to cmjohnson@faiththatconquers.com with the subject line *BOOKINGS*.

For more information OR if you are a book club, association, organization, or special interest group and you want to inquire about bulk orders, contact admin@testimonypublishersllc.online (Subject line: BULK ORDER).

DEDICATION

And forgive us our debts, as we forgive our debtors.

John 1:1, 14

I forgave.

I forgive.

I am forgiven.

Eternal and Enduring Love,

Christina M. Johnson

PUBLISHER'S NOTE

Testimony Publishers is a humble, non-traditional publishing house whose goal is to provide unique opportunities to authors who seek to compose works that encourage, motivate, empower, and inspire readers. The Testimony Publishers' family believes that everyone has a story and *CONQUEROR'S CACHE® BOOK THREE: FAITH TO FORGIVE* afforded us the opportunity to publish a fresh testimony (though packaged in the form of a daily devotional). We believe it will ignite a movement of passionate expression and purposeful reading. Like our tagline exclaims, *HISstory. HERstory. OURstory is YOURstory*™, it is our intention that you be encouraged, motivated, empowered, and inspired to express love in its highest form, share your testimony with the world, and live your best life—NOW!

Forever yours,

Testimony Publishers, LLC.

ABOUT THE CONQUEROR'S CACHE® SERIES

Dictionaries may define a *conqueror* as a *person who vanquishes; a victor*. But YHWH defines a *conqueror* as *one who overcomes tribulation, distress, persecution, famine, nakedness, peril, and the sword* (Romans 8:35-37) and *one who can never be separated from Divine Love* (Romans 8:38-39; Jeremiah 31:3). Beloved, you are reading this because **you are more than a conqueror!** You are ready to accept this mission to rescue the prisoner of war in your mind and free yourself using the resources found on these pages. *Cache* (pronounced *kash*, not *ka sha*) is a *hiding place, especially in the ground, for ammunition, food, treasure, valuables, etc.* So, the *conqueror's cache* is the WORD of Truth that is hidden in the *ground*, the *earth of your heart* (Psalm 119:11). It speaks to your conscious and subconscious minds; and others when necessary (Matthew 12:34). When warring against all foreign enemies (external) and domestic enemies (internal), the war is never *against flesh and blood* (2 Corinthians 10:4-6).

You may be wondering - *How can the WORD of Truth (scriptures, proverbs, and affirmations) fight external and internal enemies and principalities?* First, the Creator of the universe gives you the opportunity to choose: *I call heaven and earth to record this day against you, that I have set before you, life and death, blessing and cursing: therefore,* **choose life**, *that both thou and thy seed may live* (Deuteronomy 30:19). I have a choice. You have a choice, starting this very second, to choose life; for yourself and for your loved ones. Second, the Divine Promise Keeper cannot lie (Hebrews 6:18; Proverbs 30:5). The WORD, spiritual in existence, became flesh, physical in existence (John 1:1, 14). When you choose to speak life into your *dead* or mediocre circumstances and situations, you *calleth those things which be not as though they were* (Romans 4:17; Hebrews 11:3; Proverbs 18:21; John 5:21). When you choose to renew your mind and speak words of life, you make an investment in yourself, everyone around you, and your environment (Matthew 12:35-37).

CONQUEROR'S CACHE® represents your mind and heart that is filled with the WORD of Truth. It is *seasoning* for every bitter, bland, bruised, and broken condition, external and internal (Colossians 4:6; 2 Timothy 3:16). CONQUEROR'S CACHE® represents the *ammunition* (to defend against the enemy's attacks and accusations), the *food* (to nourish your conscious and subconscious minds), the *treasure* (to bless and encourage yourself and others), and a *sword* (to cut off the enemy's head). The *CONQUEROR'S CACHE®* series was made possible because of my suffering and *death* and that of those who fought by my side (Psalm 116:15). I am living proof that YHWH's WORD is true *and* that it works. It is for this reason, that I can encourage and comfort you with the same encouragement and comfort that our Faithful Creator gave to me (2 Corinthians 1:3-4).

The *CONQUEROR'S CACHE®* series is NOT about religion...

...IT IS ABOUT FREEDOM!

The *CONQUEROR'S CACHE®* series is NOT about being a Christian, Muslim, Atheist, or to argue about religion...

...IT IS ABOUT BEING FREE TO EXPRESS DIVINE PURITY, PERFECTION, PEACE, PASSION, AND PURPOSE.

In this second installment of the *CONQUEROR'S CACHE®* series, my intent and purpose are to provide encouragement, inspiration, empowerment, and motivation that will enable you to think about your own thinking; eventually, producing the by-products of Love, Peace, Joy, Harmony, Forgiveness, Health, Prosperity, and Abundance (in their highest forms).

Physical, mental, and spiritual dis-ease, thoughts and ideas of lack, and all forms of negativity *can* and *will* be vanquished! *CONQUEROR'S CACHE® BOOK THREE: FAITH TO FORGIVE* is your compact, emergency supply, and every day resource that is going to do more than help you survive. It's going to give you the key to enable you to renew your mind, heal your body, nourish your soul, and overcome your biggest challenges (Romans 12:2).

TWEET THIS! @ANOINTED_RIVER

I am more than a conqueror!

#CONQUERORSCACHE

THANK YOU FOR YOUR PURCHASE

As a small gesture of appreciation, I'd like to offer you access to:

- The CONQUEROR'S LIFE MAP Program

  Includes:

  * 11-page Workbook

  * Audio & Video Training

  * Additional worksheet and exercise that accompany the program

- And other supplemental resources and bonuses.

These companion tools will supplement the information and exercises in this one-of-a-kind devotional. I look forward to reading your comments on Amazon, Goodreads, & Instagram (**@anointed_river**), your Tweets on Twitter (**@ANOINTED_RIVER**), and your emails (**cmjohnson@faiththatconquers.com**) as you move closer to becoming a more conscious and deliberate co-creator of your reality while living your dreams!

To claim your FREE gifts, visit:

https://testimonypublishers.com/conquerorscacheresourcesandbonuses

TABLE OF CONTENTS

PART 3

PART 1

HOW TO USE THIS BOOK

The personal testimonies, scientific analyses, and spiritual revelations contained in this book can be very intensive. But, I have taken great care to divide the book into sections that can be easily, and literally processed and experienced in your conscious and subconscious minds.

Although you can start anywhere you desire and build a good foundation, I suggest that you read the entire book once; completing the metacognitive exercises at the end of each book. These metacognitive exercises incorporate cognitive dissonance and neuro-linguistic programming that you can adapt for your personal development. Subsequently, read the devotional section (Part 2) as it corresponds with the Metacognitive Realization and Habitual Re-Creation™ section (Part 3). Although this is a daily devotional, *daily* will mean something different to each reader. Although I suggest that you complete each day in order, you do not have to complete each reading or exercise before you can move on to the next. But you will find that completing and, perhaps repeating some of the readings and Metacognitive Realization and Habitual Re-Creation™ exercises will ensure immediate changes are experienced and, ultimately, become automatic. Finally, use the appendices (Part 3) to supplement and reinforce the information in Parts 1 and 2.

If you are a trainer, consultant, or coach, you will discover many ideas and exercises that can supplement and support programs, workshops, seminars, and classes that you are currently using. Explore the book and be creative with your reading experience. Each section offers a myriad of ways to incorporate and apply what you have read into your everyday life and the lives of your clients/customers/students. Refer to the **Leader's Guide (Appendix A)** for more information.

At the end of each day, you will be invited to pray. I know what you may be thinking! It's usually one of four things, *Great, I need it!* OR *Praying is too religious,* OR *I don't profess a specific, religious denomination,* OR *I'm an atheist.* But, PLEASE, DON'T SKIP THE PRAYERS!

Therefore, I say unto you, what things soever ye desire when ye pray, believe that ye receive them, and ye shall have them.
Mark 11:24

It does not matter what age, gender, race, or religion you profess, *prayer* is a means of settling your mental conflict (either marrying yourself to or divorcing yourself from the thought or idea presented). Whether you bless Yeshua HaMashiach or use the name *Jesus* or call on YHWH when you get to the crux of the matter, **every person, place,** or **thing** is a thought or an idea; and the Most-High and Sovereign Creator of Heaven and Earth knows and understands the depths of your heart.

Even when it comes to your thought and idea of Divine Expression; *prayer* is a means of communing with the Infinite Source of perfection, purity, peace, power, presence, purpose, and prosperity. The Divine Creator is Eternal Energy - always was, always has been, and always will be; can neither be created nor destroyed; can be transferred or transformed (by way of the Holy Spirit); moves in form, through form, and out of form. So, I encourage you to marry yourself to the thought and idea of your connection to the only most-high, most-pure, and most-powerful source of energy there is!

The intention of this book is to concentrate on the Cornerstone of Divine Expression and enable you to think about your thinking. The National Science Foundation says that the human brain produces between 12,000 and 60,000 thoughts per day. And what is a thought? A thought is a unit of mental energy that can be measured using scientific and spiritual apparatuses. Thought energy can be transformed into feelings, words that you speak, and actions. So, it is my intention to present you with the applicable knowledge that will help you to literally become what you think *and* do.

You will be able to re-create yourself and your environment. When you apply the information presented in the *CONQUEROR'S CACHE®* Series, changes will be immediately made in your brain. This is done by developing your FAITH, training your brain to FILTER all ideas of lack and limitation, clearing mental and spiritual limitations as you FORGIVE yourself and others, and reprograming your brain to FOCUS on all aspects of love and abundance. These changes in your thinking will re-create the very cells of your body and change the quality of your internal *and* external environments. Love, joy, peace, harmony, forgiveness, health, wealth, prosperity, and success will *be* yours.

For additional information, FREE resources, to enroll in one of the *CONQUEROR'S CACHE®* online programs, or to sign up for a CONQUEROR'S CONSULTATION, please visit https://testimonypublishers.com/conquerorscacheresourcesandbonuses or email cmjohnson@faiththatconquers.com

INTRODUCTION

Take a moment to look at yourself and around your environment. ARE YOU IN DANGER? I don't want to scare you, but, there's something you should know about unforgiveness. Many therapists and psychologist lecture individuals about the harm unforgiveness causes the mind and body. They know that living in a state of unforgiveness is dangerous to the human mind, body, and spirit.

But, what are the dangers of unforgiveness and what do you get out of forgiving your worst enemy (or enemies, if you're anything like I was). And what benefits can you expect after you forgive someone that has hurt you or someone you love?

LESSONS ON FORGIVENESS

Let me share something with you - thoughts and feelings of unforgiveness are neither empowering nor therapeutic. This is the reason knowing what it means to FORGIVE and how to use the act of forgiveness are crucial to re-creating your mindset and your reality!

And I am no stranger to trials and tribulations; pains and sufferings! Several years ago, a judge awarded full custody of my first-born son to his biological father and my husband and I suffered a miscarriage. I had two life-threatening surgeries, lost my home, my car, exited my family's transportation company, and applied for government assistance; all within a span of months.

If I knew anything at all, it was how to stay mad at someone. I knew how to hold a grudge! After all, I thought I had good reason to be angry. I was sick, tired, poor, and unhappy. I believed my family turned their backs on me and that my friends betrayed me. I had been lied on (behind my back, to my face, and in court). I was cast out, and I felt like I was *left for dead*. I was mentally and spiritually defeated; conquered. But, I learned:

FORGIVENESS
ACCELERATES YOU FROM
CONQUERED TO CONQUEROR
AND FROM VICTIM TO VICTOR!

WHAT DOES IT MEAN TO FORGIVE?

Many people live their entire lives without ever understanding forgiveness and how it enables them to access the very power of the Most-High and Omnipotent Creator. When you FORGIVE a person of their transgressions and wrongs committed against you or your loved one, you give three gifts.

The first, you access the redemptive emancipation of the Sovereign Creator and give yourself **the gift of liberty.** Second, you access the strength of the Infinite Source and give yourself **the gift of power.** And third, you access the mercy and grace of the Eternal Promise-Keeper and give your transgressor **the gift of a pardon**. And in so doing, you erase your need for an apology, payment, or service you believe may be owed to you.

For me, forgiveness meant being mentally, emotionally, and spiritually free enough to access and express the emancipation of the Sovereign Creator. It meant being empowered to access and express the strength of the Infinite Source within me. Forgiveness meant being accepting of the Eternal Promise-Keeper's gifts of mercy and grace and being able to express them to those I believed wronged me.

When you FORGIVE, you exercise and express the power of the Omnipotent Creator within you! And when the All-Intelligent and Infinite Mind lives within you, abides in you, and dwells in you, the forgiving character and nature of the Most-High and Sovereign Creator manifest victory through you!

Mercy is *not receiving the punishment and consequences that are deserved* and grace is *receiving blessings and pardons that are undeserved* (Mark 3:28, Luke 11:4, John 1:29, 1 John 1:9-10). One facet of the Sovereign Creator's expression is to remove your transgressions and wrongs AND vanquish all unrighteousness. Thereby, restoring you to your highest self. All transgressions can be forgiven; washed away and forgotten (Psalm 25:7-9, 103:9; Isaiah 1:18, 38:16-17). This is the example to follow.

When you FORGIVE, you no longer request from your transgressor that which you believe you are owed. No longer demanding an apology or confession, you have a new mindset, heart-set, spirit-set!

WHAT DOES SCIENCE SAY?

Scientific research is being carried out every day on the effects of forgiveness on the human mind and body. When you FORGIVE, science shows that the benefits are remarkable! Forgiveness lowers stress, lessens emotional reactivity, decreases suffering, increases happiness, and amplifies states of peace. For more encouragement in forgiveness, visit:

http://faiththatconquers.com/the-4-steps-to-freedom-series-part-3-forgive/

For now - let's dive in and discover how having the FAITH TO FORGIVE can change your life. And, **if you haven't already done it while reading one of the other books in this series,** I want you to make a commitment to use the 4 STEPS TO FREEDOM and the *CONQUEROR'S CACHE®* series to change your life; no matter what! If you've completed the introduction exercise, move on to part 2.

Let's get started…

TWEET THIS! @ANOINTED_RIVER

FAITH + FILTER + FORGIVE + FOCUS = FREEDOM!

#CONQUERORSCACHE

R E S P O N S * I * B I L I T Y

Introduction Exercise

So, you want to create and live a life you love? Well, let's clarify a few things. One – you *can* control the thoughts you think, the mental images that you entertain, and the actions that you carry out (the words you speak, the emotions you feel, and the behaviors you exhibit). Two – you can change your life, achieve your noblest goals, and experience your greatest dreams.

Most people choose not to control themselves and change their reality because it involves too much. Effort, time, and money are the top challenges that many men and women refuse to commit and invest in themselves and their families.

YET, HERE YOU ARE!

You have consciously decided to take responsibility for your life. You have also decided to do something different to achieve your dreams. But, let's keep this simple and clear. Before moving forward, you must do three (3) things:

A) **THE WHAT? AND THE WHEN?**
    Imagine you want to travel to Giza, Egypt. First, you must find out where you are in relation to where you want to go. Then, you can begin to plot your course.

    THE POINT: If you want to GO somewhere, anywhere, you must know where you   are and know your destination.

    EXERCISE: Write two (2) goals you want to accomplish in the next twelve (12) months. **(Column 1 of Worksheet)**

THINK ABOUT: Think about one (1) change you want to create in your life that   will help you achieve each of your goals. Write it down. **(Column 2 of Worksheet)**

Where there is no vision, the people perish:
but he that keepeth the law, happy is he.
Proverbs 29:18

B) BLAMING TO BLESSING

Do you believe there is something or someone holding you back from accomplishing your goals? What is stopping you from starting a new business, writing a book, or earning your diploma? Why haven't you achieved your ideal life, love, and happiness? Is it an unsupportive spouse, poor health, not enough money, even less time, or a lack of education and skills? Or is it the economy, "The Man," racism, sexism, ageism, or religious discrimination? Well, just as I had to find out if you believe any of that *hogwash*…YOU ARE WRONG!

THE POINT: The #1 thing holding you back from your destiny, achieving   greatness, and accomplishing your goals is YOU!

EXERCISE: Write one (1) excuse for each of your goals that you have believed in   the past to justify not creating the necessary changes to accomplish your goals. **(Column 3 of Worksheet)**

THINK ABOUT: Think about the choice or choices you made that led to your   current situation? Write it down. **(Column 4 of Worksheet)**.

Blaming other people or things is easy, but the damage that it causes is not easy to undo. Because blaming involves negative thoughts, destructive perspectives, and noxious emotions, its outcome is usually mediocrity and/or failure. In the process, people are hurt and opportunities to exhibit your highest self, are missed. However, when you bless someone or something, you think positive thoughts, create constructive perspectives, and nurture loving emotions. So, take responsibility for your thoughts, emotions, and behaviors.

But I say unto you, Love your enemies, bless them that curse you, do good to them that hate you, and pray for them which despitefully use you, and persecute you; ...
Matthew 5:44

Complete the following exercise to help you organize your thoughts. Examples have been completed to assist you.

R E S P O N S* I *B I L I T Y:

Introduction Exercise: Goals, Excuses, and Action Steps

MY GOALS	THINGS I WANT TO CHANGE	EXCUSES I'VE USED IN THE PAST	ACTIONS I MUST TAKE NOW
Example: I want to lose 20 pounds in 20 days.	How often I workout AND How much I eat after I am full	I don't have time. OR I've worked all day and should spend more time with my children.	Instead of watching TV for 2 hours after work, I am going to walk up and down my stairs for 15-minutes then take a hot bath or shower. OR I am going to dance to 4 of my favorite songs (about 20-minutes) with my children and stretch for 10-minutes afterward.
Example: I want to make a minimum of $500 dollars extra income within the next 6 months.	How many streams of income I have	The economy is terrible. OR I don't know how to earn money doing anything other than my current job.	Instead of listening to the news on my way to work, I am going to listen to an MP3 or CD working from home or earning money online. OR While I tidy up the house in the evening, I am going to listen to an audiobook on how to monetize an idea I have.
1.			
2.			

C) COMPLAINING TO COMPLIMENTING

Stop complaining! Period.

One – complaining doesn't solve any of your challenges or problems. It produces increased levels of cortisol which make you less creative and less capable of problem-solving.

Two – Complaining doesn't make you feel any better. The increased production of cortisol decreases the production of your "happy hormone," DHEA (Dehydroepiandrosterone). Low levels of DHEA are associated with accelerated aging, impaired memory, bone loss, and a reduction in muscle mass.

Instead of complaining about your life, your body, your spouse, your children, your home, your car, your job, your boss, your parents, your siblings, your in-laws, your bills, your credit cards, your student loan, your bank account balance (and whatever else you complain about), start complimenting yourself and others.

A team of Japanese scientists, led by Norihiro Sadato, has found scientific proof that a person performs better when they are complimented. A compliment is akin to receiving "a social reward of money."

THE POINT: Instead of complaining, try complimenting!

EXERCISE: When you find yourself about to complain (about anything), compliment yourself or someone else. Please, keep the compliment simple and honest. (Example: I am brilliance in action. or You did a great job, or I can draw the best stickman when I'm bored).

THINK ABOUT: Think about how often you complain about yourself and others. Think about how you feel afterward. Think about how often you compliment yourself and others. Think about how you feel afterward. Now, do the most-beneficial and most-empowering thing for yourself and others – STOP COMPLAINING AND START COMPLIMENTING!

*In everything give thanks: for this is the will of
GOD in Christ (Yeshua) concerning you.*
1 Thessalonians 5:18

R E S P O N S* **I** *B I L I T Y COMMITMENT CONTRACT

The I in RESPONS I BILITY is large because YOU play the largest part in the conquering of your mind and in the co-creation of your ideal reality. You must make the commitment to take responsibility for yourself and your future. So, as a sign of your commitment to re-creating yourself and your future, complete the following:

I, _____, commit to taking full responsibility for my thoughts, ideas, feelings, emotions, words (spoken and unspoken), and actions.

I, _____, commit to identifying my goals and desires, and making the necessary changes that will enable me to create and live my ideal reality.

I, _____, commit to turn blame into blessing by refusing to accuse someone else or something for my thoughts, ideas, feelings, emotions, words (spoken and unspoken), and actions. Instead of blaming, I will bless others, thereby freeing and empowering myself to live my best life now.

I, _____, commit to turn complaining into complimenting by refusing to complain about myself and others. Instead of complaining, I will compliment myself and others with a simple and honest statement, thereby liberating and enabling myself to re-create myself and my life.

I, _____, commit to giving my very best to participate in and complete the requirements of *CONQUEROR'S CACHE*® in such a manner that the Infinite Creator and I will be pleased with me.

_____   _____

Signature   **Date**

_____

Print Full Name

SHOW THIS CONTRACT TO A FAMILY MEMBER OR FRIEND FOR ACCOUNTABILITY PURPOSES. ALSO, EMAIL YOUR SIGNED CONTRACT TO cmjohnson@faiththatconquers.com, **subject line** *CONQUEROR'S CACHE® RESPONSIBILITY CONTRACT.*

And let us consider one another to provoke unto love and to good works...

Hebrews 10:24

NOTE: For a printable version of this contract, visit
https://testimonypublishers.com/conquerorscacheresourcesandbonuses

PART 2

FORGIVE

DAY 15:

Judge not, and ye shall not be judged: condemn not, and ye shall not be condemned: forgive, and ye shall be forgiven

Luke 6:37

Have you ever said, *I'll never FORGIVE him for what he did to me!* Or *It wasn't my fault; why should I FORGIVE her?* Or *I'm the child, they should apologize to me!* Although many people have these thoughts and ideas, they are neither empowering nor therapeutic. This is the reason knowing what it means to FORGIVE and how to use the act of forgiveness can re-create your mindset and reality. This can propel you forward and upward; from conquered to CONQUEROR!

But, what does it mean to FORGIVE?

Many people live their entire lives without ever understanding forgiveness and how it enables them to access the very power of the Most-High and Omnipotent Creator. To define the word, let's take a look at it:

For – **GIVE.**

When you FORGIVE a person of transgressions and wrongs committed, you GIVE three gifts. The first, you GIVE to yourself. It is the gift of liberty. You also GIVE yourself a second gift - power. And third, you give your transgressor the gift of a pardon. This erases your need for an apology, payment, or service you believe may be owed to you. The word *give* is extremely significant because when you

FORGIVE, you exercise and express the power of the Omnipotent Creator within you! When the All-Intelligent and Infinite Mind lives within you, abides in you, and dwells in you, the forgiving character and nature that you exhibit resembles the loving character and divine nature of the Most-High and Sovereign Creator. This loving character and divine nature are expressed in the forms of mercy and grace.

Mercy is not receiving the punishment and consequences that are deserved and *grace* is receiving blessings and pardons that are undeserved (Mark 3:28, Luke 11:4, John 1:29, 1 John 1:9-10). One facet of the Sovereign's expression is to remove your transgressions and wrongs AND to vanquish all unrighteousness. Your transgression can be forgiven; washed away and forgotten (Psalm 25:7-9, 103:9; Isaiah 1:18, 38:16-17).

When you FORGIVE, you no longer request from your transgressor that which you believe you are owed. You no longer demand an apology or confession from him/her/them and this is your new mental, emotional, and spiritual state. You also no longer desire to hurt the person or exact revenge.

Let's take another look at the word:

*F o r – g **I** v e.*

The *I* in *forgive* represents *you!* When you FORGIVE, it's ultimately for you. Forgiveness is your voluntary emancipation; willed freedom and eternal salvation because it frees and saves you. Analyze this – You already know unrighteousness (some would say, sin) lowers your vibrations and your expression of the Most-High Creator. This prevents you from your fullest expression of Eternal Love and Infinite Power. And, you already know the Creator is a part of you and you are a part of the Creator.

So, unforgiveness (a lower vibration or sin) prevents you *and* your transgressor from the expression and manifestation of the Almighty Creator. *How?* To exist in a state of unforgiveness means you are not in harmony with the Most-High and Sovereign Creator. And when you are not in harmony with the Most-High and Sovereign Creator, you are not in agreement with GOD-in-you. Therefore, your transgressor is unable to righteously connect with the manifestation and expression of the Most-High and Sovereign Source of Creation in YOU and through YOU! I don't know about you, but I no longer want to be responsible for keeping anyone from their experience with the Most-High Creator through me. (Yes, I just stated that you are at fault if you are living in a state unforgiveness.) No matter where you are on your journey of forgiveness, to overcome thoughts of unforgiveness, it's important to speak words of life into your present situation. Repeat the following positive affirmations with fervency:

I have the faith to forgive.

I am forgiven.

I forgive myself first, for every mistake, shortcoming, and failure!

I forgive myself, in truth and spirit (on my own accord) with a sound mind and a grateful heart.

I forgive every him, her, and them that hurt me with words or actions.

I am free to love, empowered to live, and deserving of every good gift from the Infinite Creator.

I am forgiveness made manifest.

For more positive affirmations, check out:

THE ABC's OF AFFIRMATIONS PROGRAM

https://testimonypublishers.com/conquerorscacheresourcesandbonuses

I read an article entitled, "Paco, All Is Forgiven." The author (P. Chircop) tells the story of a father who places an ad in the local newspaper in Madrid. It read, *Paco, meet me at the Hotel Montana at noon on Tuesday. All is forgiven! Love, Papa.* The result of this father's ad was *800 young men named Paco waiting for their fathers…and waiting for the forgiveness they never thought was possible!* Lives are touched, and relationships are healed when we FORGIVE.

You can change everything when you FORGIVE!

Let's pray.

> Infinite Forgiveness, You are All and in all. I am blessed to receive and give the gift of forgiveness. I know that when I FORGIVE, I express the very power of the Most-High and Sovereign Source of All forgiveness. When I FORGIVE, I bless You, I bless myself, and I bless everyone in existence. I am truly a master of my life when I FORGIVE. Although I may be able to remember the hurtful words, the painful situation, and the emotional depression of that hellish moment, I no longer remember what was said and done to me as torment. I no longer think thoughts that imprison me. Instead, I use my memories to name the issue and situation and then FORGIVE it. When I FORGIVE, I am free to move on, make new thoughts, and, if need be, use my old thoughts to comfort others who have gone through the same thing I did. I am empowered and unfettered. I FORGIVE in Your Forgiving Name, it is so.

Therefore, I say unto you, what things so ever ye desire, when ye pray, believe that ye receive them, and ye shall have them.

Mark 11:24

NOTES

How do you think your thoughts, words, actions, and environment will change when you forgive yourself and believe that the Most-High Creator has forgiven you?

_____

_____

_____

_____

_____

_____

_____

_____

_____

_____

_____

_____

_____

_____

_____

_____

_____

DAY 16:

Who is a GOD like unto thee, that pardoneth iniquity, and passeth by the transgression of the remnant of his heritage? he retaineth not his anger for ever, because he delighteth in mercy. He will turn again, he will have compassion upon us; he will subdue our iniquities; and thou wilt cast all their sins into the depths of the sea.

Micah 7:18-19

Let's get straight to the point today...

Abraham was an idol worshipper from Mesopotamia whom the Most-High Creator saved and blessed to be the *father of many nations*. He was divinely blessed to be the father of a holy race of believers (Genesis 12:1-3, 17:1-8; Acts 7:2-5) and he was justified by faith (Romans 4:7-9). In the book of Daniel, **King Nebuchadnezzar** was a powerful ruler who was blessed by the Most-High and Sovereign Creator to subdue many nations (including Israel) and build a vast kingdom. Because he did not acknowledge the Creator's provision of mercy and grace in his life, King Nebuchadnezzar was turned into a *birdman*. But the Forgiving Creator's loving character and divine nature expressed as *forgiveness* was exhibited after seven years when King Nebuchadnezzar was physically, mentally, and financially restored (Daniel 1:1, 2:4, 4:34-37).

Manasseh was a King of Israel who committed abominations before the Divine Creator. He was an idol worshipper, a practitioner of witchcraft, and he even murdered his children by sacrificing them to false gods. Although the Almighty gave him up, into the hands of the enemy for a time, Manasseh was restored as King of Jerusalem (2 Chronicles 33:1-16). Although most people believe **Rahab** to be a liar for protecting righteous men, the Heavenly Father did not look upon the act as a sin. Rehab was also forgiven of her sexually immoral lifestyle and blessed by the Most-High Creator to be a matriarch in the genealogy of Yeshua HaMashiach because of the *protection* she gave to righteous men (Joshua 2:1, Matthew 1:5, James 2:25). **Peter** was forgiven after, repeatedly, denying the Messiah and **Paul** (formerly known as Saul) was forgiven after persecuting YHWH's chosen people (Matthew 26:70, 72, 74-75; Mark 14:71-72, Luke 22:57-58, 60-61).

The above examples are but a few confirmations of the Most-High and Sovereign Creator's loving character and divine nature being expressed as *forgiveness*. So, believe that the Omniscient Creator knows your every trial and tribulation; all your pain and suffering. Every one of your tears is placed in the Creator's bottle and written in the Almighty's book (Psalm 39:12, 42:31, 56:8; Isaiah 38:5, 2 Kings 20:5). No matter your transgression, forgiveness is yours when you accept it.

Unlike forgiveness, unforgiveness is a prison! When you choose not to FORGIVE, you must act as judge, jury, and prison guard. You must ensure that your transgressor is not only judged, but also condemned and punished. As the expression of Perfect Forgiveness, all your battles involving unforgiveness are already won; your transgressors conquered, subdued, and destroyed! But, you must purpose to FORGIVE.

Here's your command – 1) Mark 12:30-31, *You shall* **love the LORD your GOD** *with all your heart, and with all your soul, and with all your mind, and with all your strength. The second is this, 'YOU SHALL* **LOVE YOUR NEIGHBOR AS YOURSELF.'** *There is no other commandment greater than these."* **AND** 2) Matthew 6:14-15, *For if you* **forgive others for their transgressions***, your heavenly Father will also forgive you. "But if you do not forgive others, then your Father will not forgive your transgressions.*

Finally, there is one thought that must be ever-present and exercised. What is it, you ask?

FORGIVE!

Forgive your abuser. Forgive your molester. Forgive the person who lied, cheated, stole from, and attempted to murder you. *Why?* Because when you FORGIVE, you exhibit the Infinite Power of Forgiveness and this *infinite power* releases you from the *prison of unforgiveness.*

Think about this - A judge must continuously review the transgression and pronounce the final punishment; the jury must continuously analyze and deliberate over the transgression, and a prison guard must remain *in* the prison to keep watch over the prisoner. The Creator's loving character and divine nature are expressed, most-righteously, where there is liberty and freedom from limitations.

Therefore, you express the perfect part of you, *Divine Perfection,* when you FORGIVE (Matthew 9:6; Mark 2:7, Luke 7:47; Colossians 2:13). You no longer need to over-analyze the transgression or determine what the final judgement will be. You no longer have to wallow in the hurt and lament the wrong. And you don't have to remain *in* prison to keep watch over your transgressor.

Just as Moses, in Numbers 12, forgave his sister (Miriam) for speaking against him. He spoke up for Miriam to the Almighty and requested that mercy be extended towards her. When you ask the Faithful Forgiver to FORGIVE you, He forgives you because He is faithful and just (1 John 1:9); and there is NO condemnation (Romans 8:1).

THIS IS THE PERFECT EXAMPLE!

Let's pray.

Infinite Mind, You know all my transgressions. But, I am no longer guilty because I am forgiven. I am no longer ashamed because You right my wrongs. I can now breathe because, as You promised, I am forgiven. As You promised, I am pardoned. I no longer torment myself with thoughts of hate, suicide, and death. I flood my mind and my heart with thoughts of forgiveness. I FORGIVE myself and I FORGIVE others. I am the living embodiment of Infinite Forgiveness as I renew my mind, recharge my body, and revive my spirit! I am so thankful and grateful that I am part of the energy and essence of True Forgiveness. I am Forgiveness. It is so.

NOTES

How can you express the Creator's loving character and divine nature of forgiveness over the next 3 days?

_____

_____

_____

_____

_____

_____

_____

_____

_____

_____

_____

_____

_____

_____

_____

_____

_____

_____

_____

DAY 17:

To whom ye forgive any thing, I forgive also: for if I forgave any thing, to whom I forgave it, for your sakes forgave I it in the person of Christ; Lest Satan should get an advantage of us: for we are not ignorant of his devices.

2 Corinthians 2:10-11

At the time, what happened to you may have been perceived by every sensory and processing organ in your body as a *tragedy*. However, to FORGIVE reveals Infinite Mercy and Grace in what happened to you! You must understand this — when Eternal Forgiveness is revealed to you and expressed through your conscious state of forgiveness, your desire to change or erase what happened is deleted. When you manifest Divine Forgiveness, you erase your desire to suppress and repress the heart of the matter, your thoughts & actions (and your reactions), your perpetrator's heart, and your perpetrator's thoughts & actions (and reactions). Your divine revelation will conclude:

Forgiveness changes the past, the present, and the future!
A.C. Johnson

When you FORGIVE, you get to *see* the Infinite Creator and experience the ultimate, sustaining power that carried you through your trials, tribulations, pains, and sufferings. You also get to *see* the overcoming power that allows you to stand today. That same power strengthened you when you felt weak, was a salve when you were in pain and became a comforter when you had to endure suffering; your *hell on earth* (or, if you are battling sickness in your body, your hell *in* earth)!

Take comfort in Hebrews 13:8, the Messiah *is the same yesterday, and today, and forever,* and 2 Cor 1:3-4, *Blessed be GOD, even the Father of our Lord Jesus Christ, the Father of mercies, and the GOD of all comfort; Who comforteth us in all our tribulation, that we may be able to comfort them which are in any trouble, by the comfort wherewith we ourselves are comforted of GOD.*

When you reach a state of true forgiveness, you will be able to separate your love for the divine creation (the person who hurt you) from the hurtful act of the flesh (the hurt that was carried out upon you).

FAITH TO FORGIVE

Let's take a moment to exercise:

Take a deep, heart-focused breath.

Breathe in through your nose for 2 seconds and breathe out through your mouth for 3 seconds.

Repeat 2 more times.

Just relax.

Feel your muscles relaxing; especially in your neck, shoulders, and back.

Now, say each of the following positive affirmations as naturally as you can:

I am liberated from the bondage of unforgiveness.

I am free from the heavy burden of shame and guilt.

Every chain of captivity is broken, and I am no longer embarrassed or ashamed.

I release my past mistakes, ignorance, and transgressions as I live with purity and sincerity of heart.

I am healing my mind, body, and spirit through the act of forgiveness.

I am worthy of forgiveness.

I accept my true past and FORGIVE *myself for participating in any immoral act or transgressions.*

I deserve forgiveness.

I FORGIVE *myself, once and for all.*

I am free from anger and rage as I conquer and subdue all thoughts and ideas of unforgiveness and lack.

I am compassionate and patient with others as I continuously grow in my capacity to FORGIVE*.*

Feel free to repeat these as often as you'd like;

especially when you wake up and before going to bed.

Let's pray.

Eternal and Infinite Source of my being, I am so thankful and grateful that I can see my past with Eternal and Infinite Eyes. I can see that although I may have knowingly participated in wrong-doings, I am still loved. I am still forgiven. Perfect Faithfulness is my faithfulness and Divine Forgiveness is my forgiveness. I accept my past as a part of my journey, but it does not define who I am and who I am becoming. I am a forgiver; not because I am forgiven, but because I am forgiveness. I have the Divine power to FORGIVE sins and pardon transgressions. My very nature and essence are connected to that which cannot be destroyed; that which was here since before time began. In the Name above every name, I commit my mind and heart to FORGIVE. It is so!

NOTES

Write one positive affirmation that declares your acceptance of divine forgiveness.

_____

_____

_____

_____

_____

_____

_____

_____

_____

_____

_____

_____

_____

_____

_____

_____

_____

_____

Metacognitive Realization and Habitual Re-Creation™ Exercise:

I AM ENOUGH

Today is the day that you accept two things, once and for all.

One - that you are enough!

And, two – that you are forgiven.

Today is your day!

Directions:

1. Complete this exercise by filling in the blank with your full name.
2. Paste/Tape your picture in the appropriate space.
3. Tape/Hang your completed exercise on your wall/mirror/door or any place where it will be frequently visible.
4. Read the statement at least 3 times a day; one, of which, should be spoken aloud before going to bed.
5. If you'd like a printable version of this exercise, visit:

https://testimonypublishers.com/conquerorscacheresourcesandbonuses

I, _____, am fearfully and wonderfully made to impress. I am more than a conqueror. I am loved, forgiven, and made anew. I am the temple of the Most-High Creator; re-created to express love, purity, harmony, peace, joy, perfection, forgiveness, health, wealth, prosperity, and success. I glorify the Most-High Creator with my thoughts, words, and actions. All power has been given unto me and I can do all things by the authority granted within me. I am thankful and grateful for my life. I give freely and humbly receive all that is mine. It is so!

PLACE YOUR PICTURE HERE!

I AM ENOUGH;

I AM MORE THAN ENOUGH!

DAY 18:

And oppress not the widow, nor the fatherless, the stranger, nor the poor; and let none of you imagine evil against his brother in your heart.

Zechariah 7:10

DOES THE PAST EXIST? Think about it for a moment. Here you are, present in this moment of time, space, reality; in this realm and dimension. You can mentally, physically, and spiritually participate in *this* natural moment. And I know what you're thinking – *I remember what happened like it was yesterday? When I remember what happened to me, I can even feel, taste, and smell the same things as it occurred that day! I can remember every detail of what was done to me, said to me, and remember how I felt.*

But, I ask again, DOES THE PAST EXIST?

Drumroll, please…

The answer is – The past, as it relates to the wrongs you've endured, only exists in your mind and heart!!! (Ecclesiastes 3:11) And the past only exists *if* you want it to. Let me explain.

To *exist* means *to have real being whether material or spiritual* and *to continue to be.* Many of us continue to devote the physical matter of our thoughts (in the form of our energy) and spiritual substance (in the form of our transcendent power given to us by the Most-High Creator) to living in the past. Many people allow the harmful thoughts to replay in the mind as if the event is still happening in this moment. The noxious images replay, and the toxic words echo in the mind. The very essence of one's being is murdered over and over again.

But, we've been given a divine example of what to do to rid the mind, body, and spirit of the death-producing thoughts and images of past transgressions against us. **One – FORGIVE!** When Yeshua was being crucified, he prayed for forgiveness for the world-of-transgressors (Luke 23:34). **Two – LIVE!** Although He died in *that* moment of time and space, he lives in the resurrection (Matthew 20:19, 27:46, 28:20). We, too, must be resurrected and live (John 11:25)!

We are instructed to remember the miraculous signs and wonders displayed in Ancient Egypt during the Exodus, the parting of the Red Sea, our people receiving water from a rock, manna from heaven, and so on (Exodus 14:21; 10:2; 17: 6; 16:14-15) . We are instructed to remember past transgressions and wrongs committed against us to shun and prevent the same situations and circumstances from occurring again (Deuteronomy 4:9, 6:2; Hebrews 10:32-36). But, you are **never** instructed to remember anything mentally, physically, and spiritually that torments you and keeps you in bondage. Every command and instruction from the Infinite and Sovereign Creator is to free you and enable you to live life abundantly (Isaiah 61:1; Zechariah 9:11-12; John 10:10)

So, *What does exist?*

Another drumroll, please…

The answer is – NOW!

The moment you are in 'now' exists. This is the moment of time that you must live in; being physically and mentally present in *this* moment. To be present in this moment means that you must be unbound by thoughts of lack, unmoved by thoughts of defeat, and unhindered by thoughts of unforgiveness.

As you FORGIVE, you are neither called to deny the wrong nor negate the hurt you experienced. In fact, it's necessary to remember the wrong, name it, and FORGIVE it. However, you must be willing to FORGIVE the wrong or be forever, un-righteously connected to your transgressor.

Yes, unforgiveness keeps you attached to your transgressor because it retains unhealthy thoughts, ideas, feelings, and emotions related to the wrong and the person(s) who hurt you or your loved one.

Unforgiveness also reveals that you still want something from your transgressor (an apology, a confession, or some form of payment) to compensate you for your loss, your hurt, and your pain. Living in a state of unforgiveness is spiritually equivalent to *imagining evil for your brother in your heart* (Zechariah 7:10).

So, accept *this* moment. From this moment (and I say this with Love), the physical act that caused your loss, hurt, pain, and suffering is not physically or naturally occurring in this time and space. Even if you are re-living that moment, over and over again, in your mind, take joy in knowing the you can be free from it! Even if you are still dealing with the residual effects of the transgression, in this moment, you can be free from it!

And to be free of the hurt and pain associated with your loss, suffering, or grief, you must FORGIVE. And to FORGIVE yourself and/or your transgressor(s), you must accept a mindset of thankfulness and gratefulness for your past (the good and the bad). You must accept a mindset of thankfulness and gratefulness for your present (even though you are still growing and learning through it). And you must accept a mindset of thankfulness and gratefulness for your future (accepting that it's brighter than you could ever imagine).

SAY THIS:

I am thankful and grateful for this moment!

Let's do this simple and quick exercise and notice how you think and feel (I suggest you do it at least 3 times a day for the next 3 days):

1. This exercise should only take about 1 minute (60 seconds).

2. Take a deep, heart-focused breath. Breathe in through your nose for 2 seconds and breathe out through your mouth for 3 seconds. Repeat 2 more times.

3. Just relax. Feel your muscles relaxing; especially in your neck, shoulders, and back.

4. Repeat the following statements:

   I am so thankful and grateful for this moment!

   I am so thankful and grateful for… (You fill in the rest)!

If you spend 1 minute (just 60 seconds), at least 3 times a day for the next three days, speaking thoughts of thankfulness and gratefulness,

I guarantee you'll start to think and feel differently. I believe you'll understand that you have a divine calling to be overflowing with love, joy, peace, harmony, forgiveness, health, wealth, prosperity, and success. After all, it's your destiny!

Let's pray.

> I am so thankful and grateful that I forgave. I am so thankful and grateful that I FORGIVE. I am so thankful and grateful that I am forgiven. It is so.

NOTES

I am so thankful and grateful for this moment! I am so thankful and grateful for... (Fill in the rest of the statement below to complete the exercise!)

_____

_____

_____

_____

_____

_____

_____

_____

_____

_____

_____

_____

_____

_____

_____

_____

DAY 19:

And forgive us our sins; for
we also forgive every one
that is indebted to us. And
lead us not into temptation;
but deliver us from evil.

Luke 11:4

And forgive us our debts,
as we forgive our debtors.

Matthew 6:12

I know this scripture is a bit long but stay with me for a moment. I want to review Luke 7:36-50:

> And one of the Pharisees desired him that he would eat with him. And he went into the Pharisee's house and sat down to meat. And, behold, a woman in the city, which was a sinner, when she knew that *Jesus* sat at meat in the Pharisee's house, brought an alabaster box of ointment, And stood at his feet behind *him* weeping, and began to wash his feet with tears, and did wipe *them* with the hairs of her head, and kissed his feet, and anointed *them* with the ointment. Now when the Pharisee which had bidden him saw *it*, he spake within himself, saying, This man, if he were a prophet, would have known who and what manner of woman *this is* that toucheth him: for she is a sinner. And Jesus answering said unto him, Simon, I have somewhat to say unto thee. And he saith, Master, say on. There was a certain creditor which had two debtors: the one owed five hundred pence, and the other fifty. And when they had nothing to pay, he frankly forgave them both. Tell me therefore, which of them will love him most? Simon answered and said, I suppose that *he*, to whom he forgave most. And he said unto him, Thou hast rightly judged. And he turned to the woman, and said unto Simon, Seest thou this woman? I entered into thine house, thou gavest me no water for my feet: but she hath washed my feet with tears, and wiped *them* with the hairs of her head. Thou gavest me no kiss: but this woman since the time I came in hath not ceased to kiss my feet. My head with oil thou didst not anoint: but this woman hath anointed my feet with ointment. Wherefore I say unto thee, Her sins, which are many, are forgiven; for she loved much: but to whom little is forgiven, *the same* loveth little. And he said unto her, Thy sins are forgiven. And they that sat at meat with him began to say within themselves, Who is this that forgiveth sins also? And he said to the woman, Thy faith hath saved thee; go in peace.

When you FORGIVE, you bless yourself **and** the Infinite Source of Forgiveness. You may have done a lot of things that were wrong and *out of line*. You may also have things that you did that were wrong and you believe they are *not that bad*. But, you cannot pay for any of your wrongs, in the natural present, to equate to the hurt you've caused yourself or someone in the past.

But, *blessed is he whose transgression is forgiven, whose sin is covered* (Psalm 32:1). This psalm is for me and it's for you! I beat myself up for years being overly critical and cynical. I know what unforgiveness looks and feels like. So, believe me when I tell you to stop beating yourself up for just a minute and FORGIVE yourself. When you do, you can bless yourself! If you stop acting as judge, jury, prosecutor, and prison guard over the person(s) that hurt you, you can bless yourself. You can bless the Creator and everyone around you by increasing your energy and vibrations as you FORGIVE!

Take a moment to stop stressing over what you are going to call the Messiah or what religious denomination is the best or what you will eat and drink or what you will wear. Take a moment to focus on the living example of the Messiah and implement those characteristics and the divine nature into your life. You will bless yourself and the entire universe!

> And if I say to a wicked person, 'You will surely die,' but they then turn away from their sin and do what is just and right— if they give back what they took in pledge for a loan, return what they have stolen, follow the decrees that give life, and do no evil—that person will surely live; they will not die. None of the sins that person has committed will be remembered against them. They have done what is just and right; they will surely live.
> Ezekiel 33:14-16

So, *What is forgiveness?*

FORGIVENESS IS...	FORGIVENESS IS NOT...
righteous.	unrighteous.
consideration.	forgetting.
strength.	tolerance.
respect.	condoning.
freedom.	dismissing.
peace.	reconciliation.
love.	optional.

You are promised a pardon from the Heavenly Father and are expected to express the same pardoning power. So, rejoice!

Let's pray.

> Divine Forgiver, You are faithful to FORGIVE all sins and transgressions. I am glad that I now understand what forgiveness is. At first, I just did it because I knew I had to, if I wanted to be physically, mentally, emotionally, and spiritually free. I did it because I wanted my blessings and promises. But now, I FORGIVE because it is easy! I FORGIVE because it is righteous. I see Divine Creation as perfect and I am perfect. I can see that whatever situation or circumstance I survived, endure, or will face, I already have the VICTORY and will glean from it the lessons that are necessary for my success and prosperity. I FORGIVE in the name of Ultimate Forgiveness, it is so.

NOTES

What does it mean to *FORGIVE*?

DAY 20:

Then said Jesus, Father, forgive them; for they know not what they do. And they parted his raiment, and cast lots.

Luke 23:34

YOUR PRESCRIPTION FOR FORGIVENESS:

Please read each word of the following:

I forgave. I forgive. I am forgiven. I forgave. I forgive. I am forgiven.

I forgave. I forgive. I am forgiven. I forgave. I forgive. I am forgiven.

I forgave. I forgive. I am forgiven. I forgave. I forgive. I am forgiven.

I forgave. I forgive. I am forgiven. I forgave. I forgive. I am forgiven.

I forgave. I forgive. I am forgiven. I forgave. I forgive. I am forgiven.

I forgave. I forgive. I am forgiven. I forgave. I forgive. I am forgiven.

I forgave. I forgive. I am forgiven. I forgave. I forgive. I am forgiven.

I forgave. I forgive. I am forgiven. I forgave. I forgive. I am forgiven.

I forgave. I forgive. I am forgiven. I forgave. I forgive. I am forgiven.

I forgave. I forgive. I am forgiven. I forgave. I forgive. I am forgiven.

I forgave. I forgive. I am forgiven.

"But I say to you who hear, love your enemies, do good to those who hate you, bless those who curse you, pray for those who mistreat you. "Whoever hits you on the cheek, offer him the other also; and whoever takes away your coat, do not withhold your shirt from him either. "Give to everyone who asks of you, and whoever takes away what is yours, do not demand it back. "Treat others the same way you want them to treat you. "If you love those who love you, what credit is *that* to you? For even sinners love those who love them. "If you do good to those who do good to you, what credit is *that* to you? For even sinners do the same. "If you lend to those from whom you expect to receive, what credit is *that* to you? Even sinners lend to sinners to receive back the same *amount.* "But love your enemies, and do good, and lend, expecting nothing in return; and your reward will be great, and you will be sons of the Most-High; for He, Himself is kind to ungrateful and evil *men.* "Be merciful, just as your Father is merciful.

Luke 6:27-36

It's as simple as that!

Only the strong can FORGIVE.
A.C. Johnson

Let's pray.

When I asked for forgiveness, it was granted to me! Now, without having to ask me, I FORGIVE all my transgressors. I no longer torment myself with thoughts, ideas, feelings, and emotions that are unhealthy and laced with death. I have already forgiven myself and I no longer persecute others for misunderstandings, mistakes, or out-right misdeeds against me. I am happiest when I FORGIVE. I am more loving when I FORGIVE. I am at peace when I FORGIVE. When I FORGIVE, I am doing a constructive work in my mind, body, spirit, faith, family, and finances. When I FORGIVE, I am Divine Forgiveness, it is so!

NOTES

How does forgiveness display your FAITH and strength?

DAY 21:

If we confess our sins, he is faithful and just to forgive us our sins, and to cleanse us from all unrighteousness.

1 John 1:9

After you read this paragraph, close your eyes and think of the person that hurt you the most. Remember what was said and done to you. Remember how the person's words and behaviors made you feel. Remember how the person and/or the environment smelled; remember how it looked. How did the person that hurt you or environment smell and look?

Now, close your eyes again and think of that person as a naked baby being pulled from his or her mother's womb. See the person as a baby crying with his or her arms reaching out for some loving person to hug or caress. But, he or she never receive that love or acceptance. Think of that person as a baby growing up to be an unwanted toddler and, then, a rejected child. Think of that person as a child, neglected and rushed to grow up, having to fend for him or herself. Think about that person as a creation of the Most-High Creator who has been treated as less than human; disrespected, violated, and abused.

Oh, excuse me – I apologize if I just described you.

Are you the person that hurt you the most?

Are you the person that you hate the most?

Are you the person that you can't FORGIVE?

Sometimes, the person that we cannot FORGIVE is the person that reminds us of ourselves! You hate what was said and done because you say and do the same things. Let's analyze this - everyone is not a victim (or the prey). Some people are the perpetrator (or the predator)! So, if you have them, don't cover your wrongs because **what you reveal, you heal**. You can start anew; no matter what (Psalm 32:5; Proverbs 28:13, Acts 3:19; James 5:14-16).

> But, beloved, be not ignorant of this one thing, that one day is with the Lord as a thousand years; and a thousand years as one day. **The Lord is not slack concerning his promise,** as some men count slackness; but is longsuffering to us-ward, not willing that any should perish, but that all should come to repentance.
> 2 Peter 3:8-9

I am not telling you that you must be a Christian to follow the example of the Divine Forgiver (Does this ring a bell: *Forgive them, Father, for they know not what they do?*) In fact, the word *Christian* is only used 3 times in the Bible as we know it today and pagans used the term to name believers (Acts 11:26, 26:28; 1 Peter 4:16). I am not in the habit of letting strangers walk up to my children and name them just because they don't know the name I gave them. I am also not telling you that you must be a specific denomination or any form of anything that spiritually separates you from divinely-created energies. Divine Energy is boundless and will not be limited to titles, groups, or time.

And, finally, I am not telling you that you must be a certain race; Jew, Gentile, of-color or not, original branch or grafted-in to incorporate the life lessons that are abundant in Holy Writ (Galatians 3:26-29). With approximately 50 Bibles being sold every minute worldwide, my intention is two-fold. One - that you would glean as much as possible from the testimonies and teachings of the Infinite Mind contained in the Bible. Two - that you incorporate the divine principles into your life to FORGIVE for the primary purpose of freeing yourself! I truly want you to get *there*.

> Then said Jesus to those Jews which believed on him, If ye continue in my word, *then* are ye my disciples indeed; And ye shall know the truth, and the truth shall make you free. They answered him, We be Abraham's seed, and were never in bondage to any man: how savest thou, Ye shall be made free? Jesus answered them, Verily, verily, I say unto you, Whosoever committeth sin is the servant of sin. And the servant abideth not in the house for ever: *but* the Son abideth ever. If the Son, therefore, shall make you free, ye shall be free indeed.   John 8:31-36

Let's pray.

Wait a moment - today, we're going to do something different!!!

I know, you can't wait to find out what it is.

Wait for it…

…wait for it…

…OK –

SAY THIS:

I already know that I am forgiven. So, today, I am not going to pray for myself. I am going to pray for _____ .

Now, you must fill in the blank. And you can't fill in the blank with the person who cut in front of you in the grocery store line. And you can't fill in the blank with a person who you have already forgiven.

YOU HAVE TO FILL IN THE BLANK WITH A PERSON YOU CONSIDER AN ENEMY WHO HURT YOU; A CRIMINAL WHO SHOULD BE IN JAIL FOR WHAT THEY DID TO YOU; A DEMON IN THE FLESH THAT HAS NOTHING BUT ILL-WILL, FIERY DARTS, DAMNATION, AND DESTRUCTION INTENDED FOR YOU.

Are you ready?

Take a deep, heart-focused breath. Breathe in through your nose for 2 seconds and breathe out through your mouth for 3 seconds.

Repeat 2 more times.

Just relax and feel your muscles relaxing; especially in your neck, shoulders, and back.

Do you have that person's name on your tongue and face pictured in your mind?

Let's pray.

> I am praying for _____. I know that _____ needs Divine Love and unceasing prayer. I do not dismiss nor condone what was said and done to me by _____, but I know that there is a lesson in the situation that has made me stronger and more enlightened. _____ was fully aware of what he/she said and did to me. But not forgiving _____, is not an option for me. Because I am a forgiver, I pray for _____'s happiness. I pray for _____ and that Eternal Love will overflow in his/her life. I pray that peace and joy will fill _____'s mind and heart. I know that my prayers settle all mental and spiritual conflict within me about _____. So, the matter is settled in my mind and heart. My authority and energy will chase away all darkness and lack and produce the brightest light and abundance. I know that there is a divine plan for _____'s life and I pray that True Love will work in his/her life! I know, believe, and accept, it is so!

NOTES

How do you honestly feel now that you have forgiven someone you considered an enemy who hurt you?

_____

_____

_____

_____

_____

_____

_____

_____

_____

_____

_____

_____

_____

_____

_____

_____

_____

_____

TWEET THIS! @ANOINTED_RIVER

I AM MORE THAN ENOUGH!

#CONQUERORSCACHE

PART 3

APPENDICES

APPENDIX A

METACOGNITIVE REALIZATION AND HABITUAL
RE-CREATION™: A BRIEF OVERVIEW

Scientific research on the brain is ever-increasing! In the past, it was believed that the human brain was static (meaning *lacking the ability to develop*) and unchanging. However, today, more information is being presented to show that the human brain is plastic (malleable) and capable of physically, chemically, and functionally changing. The brain recovers from a myriad of disease and trauma. It can also repair and restructure itself. The brain can also regain and increase its functionality. Simply stated, the human brain *can* change!

Scientific research on the imagination and the brain indicate that imagining (using the human imagination) and doing (physically, mentally, and emotionally carrying out actions) engage the same neural pathways and are influenced by each other. The same connection between the brain and the nervous system are used when you **imagine doing** something and when you **do** that same something. Simply stated, using your imagination to see, feel, and experience something creates the same brain function as physically carrying out that action.

SO, WHAT IS METACOGNITIVE REALIZATION & HABITUAL RE-CREATION™?

Metacognitive Realization and Habitual Re-Creation™ is a process involving a specialized form of meditative prayer. It enables you to become fully aware of your mental actions and the processes of acquiring knowledge and understanding by means of your thoughts, senses, experiences, and environment. It enables you to constantly create new mental, physical, emotional, and spiritual realities that intensify spiritual communion with the Most-High GOD while increasing comfort, heightening awareness, increasing F.O.C.U.S., restoring balance, and producing your ideal concepts.

Simply stated, Metacognitive Realization and Habitual Re-Creation™ helps you *think about your thinking*. Thinking about your thoughts and ideas enable you to become aware of your negative and unrighteous thoughts. Negative and unrighteous thoughts are based on hate, fear, doubt, worry, unforgiveness, bitterness, lack, contention, sickness, and poverty.

When you become aware of these destructive and death-producing thoughts and ideas, you can remove them and replace them with thoughts and ideas of love, trust, peace, forgiveness, kindness, abundance, harmony, healthiness, and prosperity. When you become aware of what thoughts and ideas to remove and replace, you can, then, construct (or re-create) a mental, physical, emotional, spiritual, and financial state that manifests your ideal reality.

Metacognitive Realization and Habitual Re-Creation™ is based on the following scriptures:

> **1 Thessalonians 5:17**, *Pray **without** ceasing.*

> **Deuteronomy 30:19,** *I call heaven and earth to record this day against you, that I have set before you life and death, blessing and cursing: therefore **choose life**, that both thou and thy seed may live:*

> **Romans 12:2,** *And be not conformed to this world: but be ye transformed by the **renewing of your mind**, that ye may prove what is that good, and acceptable, and perfect, will of God.*

It is the only method of meditative prayer based on the WORD of Truth, prayers, meditations, testimonies, proverbs, positive affirmations, universal spiritual principles, and scientific laws. It is founded on the idea of becoming a new creation by the renewal of your mind. It also incorporates heart-focused, rhythmic breathing, thought realization and retrieval, prophetic visualization, and positive affirmations.

Metacognitive Realization and Habitual Re-Creation™ is a meditative form of prayer that utilizes a four-step model: Faith, Filter, Forgive, and Focus. It is one of the quickest modalities to achieve clarity and realization while enabling the conscious mind to think positive, constructive, and life-producing thoughts (and experience the corresponding feelings) and the subconscious mind to accept one's divine identity and the promises of the Most-High Creator, according to the scriptures.

THE PURPOSE OF METACOGNITIVE REALIZATION & HABITUAL RE-CREATION™

With new, scientific research, paired with what we know about the power of prayer and believing, Metacognitive Realization and Habitual Re-Creation™ was crafted! The main purposes of Metacognitive Realization and Habitual Re-Creation™ is:

1. To allow one to go beyond human consciousness and enter the subconscious mind to identify the thoughts, ideas, feelings, and emotions (Metacognitive Realization) of hate, lack,

unforgiveness, dis-ease, failure, etc. After which, there are constant reprogramming of human thoughts, ideas, feelings, and emotions (Habitual Re-Creation) to produce love, abundance, forgiveness, health, success, etc.

2. To mentally rehearse one's desires, ideal reality, and lifestyle until one transcends time and space (as units and dimensions of measurement). This will enable one to emotionally experience one's true desires, ideal reality and lifestyle until all suppressed, repressed, and depressed energy is liberated. This will enable one to appear as one's true and highest self and express the Most-High Creator through one's thoughts, words, and actions. And,

3. To create automatic, unconscious habits of mind that produce mental processes and activities that create life and love to manifest one's desires, ideal reality, and lifestyle.

SO, WHAT DOES THAT MEAN?

Metacognitive Realization and Habitual Re-Creation™ enables you, NOT only to meditate but to become MEDITATIVE. Becoming *meditative* means you won't have to stop, set aside an hour, find a *perfect* place, change your clothes, or get a mat. It enables you (right when you need it and right where you are) to incorporate the four-step method into your lifestyle. Whatever time of day, wherever you are, and in 3-7 minutes, relax, relieve tension, gain clarity, increase creativity, and F.O.C.U.S.

You need an instructor for most meditation methods. And if your life is demanding or others are depending on you because you are the head of your household, the backbone of your company, or you make decisions that affect a lot of people/families, you have to incorporate this meditative praying style into your day. But how and why? To do what you do, day-in-and-day-out, you must have strong FAITH or develop the FAITH that you already have. It is necessary for you to be able to identify and FILTER negativity, destructive thoughts, and unhealthy emotions. You must be able to FORGIVE those who've wronged you so that you can let go of all the baggage that comes with unforgiveness and move forward; upward to your highest self. And, you absolutely, must be able to F.O.C.U.S. on positive, constructive, and life-producing thoughts and emotions.

COMMON MISCONCEPTIONS ASSOCIATED WITH MEDITATIVE METHODS THAT DO NOT APPLY TO

METACOGNITIVE REALIZATION & HABITUAL RE-CREATION™

1. You will lose control of your mind or allow evil spirits/energy to enter you.

You will **not** *lose control of your mind* or *allow evil spirits/energy to enter you.* Metacognitive Realization and Habitual Re-Creation™ purposes for you to gain greater awareness and control over your thoughts, ideas, conscious mind, and subconscious. This will lead to your ability to control your feelings and emotions; and, then, your environment and reality!

2. It is difficult to do.

It is **not** *difficult.* Because Metacognitive Realization and Habitual Re-Creation™ enables you to concentrate and focus on what is, absolutely, necessary, you can complete most of the exercises in 3 to 7 minutes. When you are tired of living a life devoid of peace, passion, purpose, purity, prosperity, provision, and power, 3 to 7 minutes is easy!

3. It takes too long to learn the method and techniques.

It does **not** *take too long to learn the methods and techniques.* You are guided through the method and technique. When you are ready to practice independently, you will be comfortable and confident!

4. It is based on some occult or false religion.

It is **not** *based on some occult or false religion.* Unlike many meditative methods, Metacognitive Realization and Habitual Re-Creation™ is not based on religion. However, it is important to be very clear that our meditations, affirmations, and visualizations *are* based on the scripture, ancient proverbs, positive affirmations, universal spiritual principles, and scientific laws as inspired by the Divine Creator!

Although many are practicing Yoga (based on Hindu Religious Worship) and Pole Dancing Workouts (based on the sexually immoral orgies, prostitution, and Asherah pole worship), Metacognitive Realization and Habitual Re-Creation™ is transparent as you are made fully aware, from the very beginning, that you *are* participating a meditative method that incorporates Old & New Testament scripture, ancient proverbs, positive affirmations, universal spiritual principles, and scientific laws. And, though, this is true, this meditative method

does not intend to instruct or require anyone to become part of any form of religion.

For your preview of Metacognitive Realization and Habitual Re-Creation™ and to supplement your reading of the *CONQUEROR'S CACHE*® Series, you complete four exercises (Refer to Appendix B). One exercise will follow each of the 4 STEPS TO FREEDOM (FAITH, Days 1-7: Exercise 1; FILTER, Days 8-14: Exercise 2; FORGIVE, Days 15-21: Exercise 3; and F.O.C.U.S., Days 22-28: Exercise 4). The exercises are intended to assist you as you *think about your thinking* and help you reflect on your thoughts and feelings, release destructive and unhealthy thoughts and feelings, and restore your thought-life to a life-producing and reality-changing focus.

And, finally, you will be guided through an Introductory 3-Minute Meditative Session. This guided session will help you increase relaxation, reduce stress, accelerate learning, and enhance creativity while focusing on life-producing thoughts. This will, ultimately, help you decrease negative thoughts and feelings, increase your energy and vibration, and identify the next steps to take or the idea that is going to create passive income or a myriad of other things.

THE MAIN GOALS OF METACOGNITIVE REALIZATION AND HABITUAL RE-CREATION™

The short-term goal of this meditative method is to create new neural pathways (brain connections/thoughts) that enable you to reflect on your thoughts and ideas, be present and grateful in the current moment, and experience (and process) your future before it occurs.

The long-term goal of this meditative method is to maintain the new neural pathways that are based on love, trust, peace, forgiveness, kindness, abundance, harmony, healthiness, and prosperity. These virtuous thoughts and ideas lead to affirmative feelings and emotions that manifest as effectual actions and behaviors.

Metacognitive Realization and Habitual Re-Creation™ offers a solution; an answer to hate, doubt, worry, unforgiveness, discord, sickness, lack, and poverty. And, most importantly, the solution, the answer is based on THE ROCK!

Let's begin by meditating on & completing the following exercise:

1. Are your thoughts filled with ungodly F.E.A.R. (**Fiction Embraced As Reality**), hate, doubt, worry, unforgiveness, bitterness, lack, contention, sickness, and poverty?

When your conscious and subconscious minds are filled with destructive and death-producing thoughts, the effects are lethal!

THOUGHTS	EFFECT
• I can't do this. • This won't work. • I don't have enough.	**Inaction** – You talk yourself out of it
• I'll try it. • What if this doesn't work. • If I don't make it, it must be God's will.	**Inefficient Action** – You procrastinate or produce a mediocre outcome, product, or service

2. Are your thoughts filled with faith and confidence; Godly F.E.A.R. (**F**aith **E**nsures **A**wesome **R**esults), love, trust, peace, forgiveness, kindness, abundance, harmony, healthiness, and prosperity?

When your conscious and subconscious minds are filled with constructive and life-producing thoughts, the effects are beneficial!

THOUGHTS	EFFECT
• I am unstoppable! • I am fully committed to accomplishing my dreams! • I have everything I need to be successful!	Action – You speak those things that aren't as though they are and produce a glorifying outcome

3. Identify the one (1) thought that you have most throughout the day. If the thought is related to some form of ungodly F.E.A.R. (hate, doubt, worry, unworthiness, unforgiveness, temptation, etc.) think of (and write down) one (1) positive AFFIRMATION or biblical promise that reflect the TRUTH of the Most-High GOD for yourself and your life. Refer to the following table to assist you:

THOUGHT RELATED TO...	TRUTH/PROMISE OF THE MOST-HIGH CREATOR
...fear.	<ul><li>God has not given me the spirit of fear.</li><li>I am Love.</li><li>I have power.</li><li>I have a sound mind.</li><li>I am more than a conqueror.</li></ul>
...doubt.	<ul><li>I trust in the Infinite Creator with all my heart.</li><li>I am wise, and my steps are divinely ordered.</li><li>I am confident that my decision is sound.</li><li>I am assertive and assured.</li></ul>
...unworthiness.	<ul><li>I was created to express and glorify the Most-High Creator.</li><li>I am the Most-High's workmanship and I am worth dying for.</li><li>I am worthy of love, peace, and joy.</li></ul>
...low self-image/esteem /worth.	<ul><li>I am all-together beautiful and there is no flaw in me.</li><li>I am perfect and holy.</li><li>I am in love with myself.</li><li>I show others how to treat me by being kind and loving to myself.</li></ul>
...hate.	<ul><li>The Creator is Love.</li><li>I am the Creator's temple and habitation.</li><li>I am Love and I love all.</li></ul>
...sickness.	<ul><li>I am a Divine Healer.</li><li>I have the power to heal the sick, give the gift of Life, and express the perfection of the Divine Healer in my mind, body, spirit, and finances.</li><li>I am healthy and strong.</li></ul>
...worry.	<ul><li>I am anxious for nothing.</li><li>I embody the peace that surpasses ALL understanding.</li><li>I am calm, composed, and content.</li></ul>

LEADER'S GUIDE

If you are a leader, trainer, consultant, or coach, you are doing a constructive work in the minds, hearts, and lives of divine creations of the Most-High Creator. In addition to understanding one's true identity, it is a life-changing experience to know who you are as the Infinite Creator intended. And what's more, to believe the divine promises of love, health, wealth, forgiveness, abundance, peace, and success are your right-now inheritances is liberating.

It is for this reason, that I have included a FREE Leader's Guide that offers suggestions, discussions, and activities to assist you as you serve others by leading.

Please visit

https://testimonypublishers.com/conquerorscacheresourcesandbonuses to access your FREE Leader's Guide and to purchase the complete guide. If you have any questions or concerns, please write to comments@faiththatconquers.com.

METACOGNITIVE REALIZATION AND HABITUAL RE-CREATION™
INTRODUCTORY 3-MINUTE MEDITATIVE SESSION

- Relax
- 3-Deep, Heart-Focused Breathes
- FAITH
  The Most-High
  Me
  My World
- FILTER
  (Choose any 3 per session)
  Faith, Family/Friends, Finances, Food, Fitness, Fun, Future
- FORGIVE
  Myself
  Person #1
  Person #2
- FOCUS
  Thankful & Grateful
  The Truth About Me
  The Truth About My Life/World
- CLOSING STATEMENT
  Today is the BEST day of my life!

NOTE: Please visit https://testimonypublishers.com/conquerorscacheresourcesandbonuses to access your 3-Minute Meditative Training Session.

WIN!

FREE RESOURCES!

Testimony Publishers, LLC. and the creators of the *CONQUEROR'S CACHE*® series have teamed up to offer our readers a chance to win metacognitive MP3 audio programs, eCourses, online trainings, and self-help books (all designed, specifically, for the reader that desires a life overflowing with love, joy, peace, harmony, health, wealth, and prosperity).

For your chance to win, simply clip this entry form*, enter your information and send to:

Testimony Publishers, LLC.: FREE RESOURCES

PO BOX 2869

Jackson, WY 83001

----

*Must be completed.

NAME*: _____

ADDRESS*: _____

CITY*: _____STATE: _____

ZIP CODE*: _____

EMAIL*: _____

PHONE (Optional): _____

**Only original entry form will be accepted. Must be 18 years or older to apply.*

APPENDIX B

METACOGNITIVE REALIZATION AND HABITUAL RE-CREATION™
REFLECT, RELEASE, AND RESTORE EXERCISES

Congratulations! You are on your way to becoming a more conscious and deliberate co-creator of your ideal reality. That's why I've included supplemental metacognitive exercises that will enable you to think about your thinking. As you complete each exercise, you will be able to make the necessary changes that will accelerate you forward and upward!

Please visit

https://testimonypublishers.com/conquerorscacheresourcesandbonuses to access your FREE "Reflect, Release, and Restore" Exercises and start living a victorious life now! If you have any questions or concerns, please write to comments@faiththatconquers.com.

Complete BOOK THREE'S Exercise (FORGIVE)

WORKS CITED

Hill, Napoleon et. al. 2007. *The Prosperity Bible*. New York: Jeremy P. Tarcher/Penguin.

Holy Bible: Authorized King James Version. Philadelphia: National Pub. 1978.

Lockman Foundation, The. 1981. *The Strongest NASB's Exhaustive Concordance*. Grand Rapids: Zondervan.

Napoleon Hill Foundation, The. 2011. *Outwitting the Devil*. New York: Sterling Publishing.

Peale, Norman Vincent. 2003. *The Power of Positive Thinking*. New York: Touchstone.

Random House Webster's Unabridged Dictionary. 2001. New York: Random House Reference.

ABOUT THE AUTHOR

Christina M. Johnson was born and raised in Baltimore City, Maryland. She was educated in the Baltimore City Public School System and completed her Bachelor of Science degree in Biology (with a concentration in Chemistry and Secondary Education). After living in Petach Tikvah, Israel, where she researched Human T-Cell Lymphotrophic Virus Type-1 at the Rabin Medical Center, she returned to the United States of America with a desire to educate. In addition to her divine calling to share her testimony and educate, she became a professional hair and make-up model for Colomer (Revlon's former parent company). She also attended Johns Hopkins University (for graduate studies in Reading Instruction) while gaining teaching experience in the same public-school system where she was educated and at a renowned private school in the area. She assisted several school administrations to develop a curriculum specifically for the youth, young adult, and at-risk communities. After focusing on growing her family, she and her husband, A.C. Johnson received the divine calling to start a boutique publishing company and author a series of metacognitive devotionals entitled, *CONQUEROR'S CACHE®.* *CONQUEROR'S CACHE®* teaches readers how to develop a faith that conquers lack, dis-ease, poverty, and failure while enabling them to express abundance, health, prosperity, and success in their lives. Incorporating her studies in biology and chemistry, along with her coursework in secondary education and instructional reading, she has a passion to explain the biological and physiological processes involved in the regeneration of the human brain, the renewing of the human mind, and its connection to the spirit. She is also the creator of the *EZ-PZ Authorpreneur*™ **Program** that teaches everyday people how to plan, publish, and profit from their transformational book. Known as *The Lady Authorpreneur*, Christina M. Johnson is a writer, author, certified trainer, transformation consultant, and entrepreneur who has written and produced scientific articles, curricula, original short stories, stage plays, and books.

THE CONQUEROR'S CACHE® SERIES

I pray you've enjoyed and benefited from reading this selection. **Please leave a sincere comment on Amazon, Goodreads, and your social media accounts**. I thank you in advance for your comment(s)! Also, if you haven't already done so, I invite you to experience the entire *CONQUEROR'S CACHE®* series:

Book One: Faith that Conquers

Book Two: Filter Your Faith

Book Three: Faith to Forgive

Book Four: Faith to F.O.C.U.S. (Focus On Conquering Until Successful)

TESTIMONY PUBLISHERS SURVEY

Dear Reader,

Testimony Publishers, LLC. would love to be your "go-to" publishing house for all your publishing needs. But we need to know more about you, what you want to read, and what you need help with. Just complete the following for amazing opportunities:

A. VISIT: https://linktr.ee/anointed_river
B. FOLLOW Christina M. Johnson on Twitter @ANOINTED_RIVER & Instagram @anointed_river.
C. TWEET and POST a picture of your copy of *CONQUEROR'S CACHE*® using our hashtag, #CONQUERORSCACHE (you may appear in the picture if you choose) - AND- SHARE how this book has helped you or what you want to read more of. You will automatically be entered in our giveaway for a Testimony Publishers' **CONQUER-cation** (or our current giveaway)! A *CONQUER-cation* is an **all-expense paid, 3-days/2-nights vacation** where you will be able to RELAX, RECHARGE, READ your favorite book, and, most-importantly, begin to RE-CREATE your life's vision & goals.   - AND -
D. (A) FILL out the entry form below.
    (B) MAIL it to the address shown. You will automatically receive **FREE RESOURCES** from Testimony Publishers, LLC. and the CONQUEROR'S CACHE® Team.

Thank you in advance for helping us serve you. Now, simply send the entry form to:

Testimony Publishers, LLC.

PO BOX 2869

Jackson, WY 83001

Testimony Publishers, LLC.: GIVEAWAY

*Must be completed.

NAME*: _____

ADDRESS*: _____

CITY*: _____ STATE*: _____

ZIP CODE*: _____ EMAIL*: _____

PHONE (Optional): _____

Are you a writer or an author who needs publishing assistance OR would you like to specify your desired content/genre?

_____

NOTE: Only original entry form will be accepted. Must be 21 years or older to apply.

Lightning Source UK Ltd.
Milton Keynes UK
UKHW01f1825280618

324950UK00001B/148/P